WHEN WORDS FAIL

PUJITA GANOTRA

Copyright © Pujita Ganotra 2024
All Rights Reserved.

ISBN

Hardcase 979-8-89610-796-5
Paperback 979-8-89610-356-1

This book has been published with all efforts taken to make the material error-free after the consent of the author. However, the author and the publisher do not assume and hereby disclaim any liability to any party for any loss, damage, or disruption caused by errors or omissions, whether such errors or omissions result from negligence, accident, or any other cause.

While every effort has been made to avoid any mistake or omission, this publication is being sold on the condition and understanding that neither the author nor the publishers or printers would be liable in any manner to any person by reason of any mistake or omission in this publication or for any action taken or omitted to be taken or advice rendered or accepted on the basis of this work. For any defect in printing or binding the publishers will be liable only to replace the defective copy by another copy of this work then available.

Contents

Hardest Goodbye

It is scary, you know
Watch them go
We stand at the airport
With full packed bags and half our soul

Memories flood my mind
You know, the deadly kind
All the times we laughed
All the times we cried
When I felt scared in the dark
You held me through the night.

We have had our ups
We have had our downs
We 've shared hysterical laughter
We've shared frowns

We were always the talk of the town
We grew up together, you know
We have bled and we have grown
We have been pushed
We have been thrown
How else could we have grown?

We have been labelled a thousand times
We have listened to insults that might even rhyme
But we held our heads high
Not showing how much, we have cried.
I mean it is hard you know
I want you to grow
But I cannot seem to let you go.

It is a strange feeling
I guess I will be reeling
From your absence from our childhood house.
Where once lived two kids, a husband, and his spouse.

I guess I'll remember our favourite couch
My dad jokes and your typical nose scrunch
Our late-night conversations
Our afternoon brunch
Everything will stop
Here I will be, completely undone.

Now the pain gushes through my eyes
The bottled-up tears flow through my face.
My knees give out.
I resist the urge to shout
And say- "Come back, don't leave me here."
Instead, I give you a teary smile.
A promise to stand back here.

To stand on the sidelines and cheer.
I say -
"No matter where you go
No matter how much you grow.
I'll love you no matter what
I hope you remember me in your thoughts."

Unveiling the Mask

I am afraid that one day they all are going to see me the way I see myself
They will finally notice the scars on my body
That I am yet to mend

I guess I do not know what I feel
I will just peel the remaining parts
Of the person that I used to be
Now all I want to do is scream
Guilt free happiness seems like a dream

I have worn this mask
Every second
Everyday
Being the nice kid
I do not have a say

All I must be is polite
While I remain oblivious from my family's sight
Yeah, I have always been this uptight

I am like a ticking bomb like I'm going to burst any day
And surprisingly I dream of that day

When they see my pent-up emotion
My mind's continuous state of commotion
The fear of not having control
The role of the eldest daughter I uphold

Now I'm staring at the ceiling
Wondering if it ever will be okay
Wondering if I'll ever fulfil my dreams
Or will I feel this blue each and every day

A short break would be fine
For this damn head of mine
For once I want to shine
For once I want to unleash the pain
That's been hiding behind my smile

Is growing up meant to hurt so much?
To balance between protecting personal space
And craving human touch
I'm just sensitive behind a temperament so rough

My mind is like an old door
Whenever someone tries to enter, I fold
At least that's what I've been told

So, I lean towards art
I pour my complete heart
My anxiety
My pain

My fear of ending up alone and disdain
I feel chained
Yet I wake up every morning like I've been trained.

I pull up my hair into a makeshift ponytail
I put my mask on
I give myself no option to fail
I close my eyes
I mentally count all the ways my life would derail
All the ways I would fail
I plop back into my bed
While my neck creeps with dread
I wish I could live in this sanctuary
Just me and my emotions best left unshed

The Unspoken Pain

Disfigured body
Freckles on her nose
She lives her life on tip toes

She's Taylor Swift's Mirrorball
She's the inspiration behind Nothing new
She feels so lonely inside
No one has a single clue

She has no idea
Where her life's going to go
Will she be a loser forever?
Will she ever become the star of her own show?

Is she forever going to bleed?
Is she ever going to grow?
Is it ever going to be easier for her?
Is she ever going to feel at peace?
Is she ever going to become a plant?
Will she forever remain a seed?

So, she goes to the one place
She lets herself feel

Where she gives herself the false hope
That one day she is going to heal

But she knows that it is an escape
And at the end of the day
She must be back
To her life as a lonely sack

She's got to pay the bills
Survive through life in the name of thrill
Where she pretends to be okay
When she feels living is like a drill

Like she feels like life's a party
And she feels like a total buzzkill
Like she doesn't know the definitions of words such as
'chill' and 'ease'
Well, how could she?
When she never feels at peace

So, she goes to her second place of refuge
Where no one asks for any explanation
No unnecessary quest for the truth
Where she can cry
As much as she wants
She won't hear her mother's criticism and taunts

She can cry away her pain
Her worries

Her imperfect stains
Her scars
Are only visible to the stars
Who does not advise or complain
They just listen to her pain

Between the Pages: A Quiet Rebellion

They say don't just stay in the corner
Come out and have fun
Don't hide behind your bookshelf
Learn to ask for help

Stop being so boring
Come out of your shell
You can leave the room if you've got nothing to tell

So, I just do that but stop at the doorframe
I wonder why the other kids and I can't be the same.
At this realisation, tears prickle my eyes
Gosh why can't they understand that I've honestly tried?

I went to a party, you know
There were all kids with whom I grew
They were laughing and joking around
I was just there, awkward, making no sound

Then I went to the library
Bought a book on how to be cool
Apparently buying a book about it made me seem like a tool

But I didn't give up
I wanted to be the girl whom they considered 'cool'
I changed all my wardrobe
I changed all my clothes
I tried to be the girl who talks

I'm the quiet kid
You must've gathered as much
The girl who's never included
I guess that's what made me too secluded

Don't even start about the birthdays
Because they are the worst
When you're not even anyone's priorities
Not second and not even third

I mean it happens, you know
When you kind of grow
You've got to be interesting
But it's all for the show

So, I stay away from the mean girls with the perfect curls
Just the thought of talking to them makes my stomach churn
But they've got these thin bodies and cheeks that glow
Meanwhile I stare from the corner like the side character
in her own show

So where do I go?
I ask myself

Since I have already established
That I don't ask for help

I go to the one place that doesn't judge
This place is like my only home
In the world that stares and compares
Books have always been there
From being a kid to a teen to an adult
They've always made me feel loved

So, I stay right there
Between the dark wooden isles
I guess I've always been there
Ever since I was a child

So, it is safe to say that I will not come out
I will stay here to scream and shout
For I will not let them see the effect they have on me
I would rather stay in this world of make believe

Rebel's Resolve

"What are you most scared of?"
They asked
"Failure" she answered
For she had forgone her mask

She promised to herself
She won't be the person she used to be
The girl who stayed quiet
When all she wanted was to scream

Her thoughts were loud
So was her self-doubt
She felt messed up inside
She felt as if a part of her died

Tried, she genuinely tried
To be the perfect daughter
The perfect bride
But alas! She failed
Her reputation's stained

People whispered
People talked

About the girl distraught
But this time she fought

She cried and cried at first
Then she started having this thirst
Of freedom and revenge
This time she decided it was society that had to bend

The first step was to do anything but blend
Ironic! Am I right?
The girl was crazy enough to think
That she could fight
The society and their rules
She refused herself to be their tool

Day and night
She would prepare
For their judgemental stares

She looked in the mirror
And practiced a lot
To keep her confidence high
Not to react to their pitiful sighs

It took a lot of time
Undo the damage, they had caused
Sometimes slow down and even pause

But she didn't give up
She fell and stood back up
She wanted to become tough

This went on for days to weeks to months
For life never stops for anyone
She fought and she fought well
She made sure to leave a legacy
Worthy to be called a rebel

Dear Mother

Dear Mother, do you not love me anymore?
I ask this question in my head
As I stare at your closed door

I tear my gaze from the door
I start having conversations with ghosts on the same floor
I ask them if they see it too.

They tilt their head, feeling muddled
They think I'm troubled
I shake my head and try to explain
How our relationship shifted from love to disdain

Remember mum when I was six?
Whatever we did, we would just instantly click
We laughed
We cried
But I guess that story died

Remember Mum?
When I was seven
You introduced me to Heaven
Ok! Maybe It's an exaggeration
But tell that to my imagination

My first visit to a bookstore
Remember, how I gaped as we walked through the door?
You told about all the books that you had read
Yes, I remember every word that you said

We walked through the wooden isles
We were all sunshine and smiles
You bought me my first book that day
I repeat that day in my mind all night and day

Seasons changed
So did you
I don't know which version of you is true

The one that laughed and teased
Or who scowls at me by my mere sight
The one who danced with glee
Or the woman who would never be pleased

Silent tears roll down my cheek
How did our lives become so colourless and bleak?
From being best friends
We became two people who do not even speak

Behind me I hear my bedroom door creak
I can feel my little brother peek
But the tears don't stop
I'm almost tempted to ask him to bring a mop

I cry for the person my mom was
I cry because I'm a lost cause
I cry for what we were
I cry for what we could have become

But the woman who was warmth is gone
Our relationship worned off and torn
So, I wipe my tear-streaked cheeks
And move towards the door that creaks

For my pillows will hear my pain
Because they don't mind
When I complain
I pray for the rain to come
For here I lie, undone

Dear Brother

Dear brother
Do you know?
How much I would love to see you grow?
But I kind of don't want to watch you go?

It sucks, you know!
When they talk about you leaving
I can hear my heart tearing

We were something, weren't we?
A duo who doesn't much speak
We had an understanding, I guess
Your presence felt like a caress

It's the older sibling syndrome that we share
We don't talk much
But we care
We learnt to lift our heads up in a room full of glares

I try to remember a time when we were just kids
No responsibility
No desire to fit
No fear that we would drift

Strawberry jelly and ice cream cones
Plastic tents and made-up homes
These are the memories I want to hold
When we have kids to getting old

Time flies by so fast
Within a blink of an eye
We grow up so fast!

One minute we're starting at the stars that glow
Then in the next, we brace ourselves for the challenges
that life might throw

Getting ready for school to getting ready for a job
interview
You really grew
You're so much more than that subdued kid
I am so grateful for everything you did

You were security
You were warmth
You were the role model
I didn't realise I'd want

It hurts when one bird flies and the other
stays behind
But alas! That is life
One day you fear the dark
Then the other day you have found the strength to
survive

One day you will have everything you want
You will just have to figure out what you desire
If not a winner, I still grew up with a trier.

Dear brother
Remember our hugs
Remember our frowns
Remember us in your ups and downs
In the towns that you will live
Remember there is still a home where you can still be a kid

Will I?

Every night when I lay in bed
Filled with a thousand questions in my head
Will I ever be happy?
Will I ever be strong?

But the question that keeps me up all night
Is whether this chaos will ever end,
Would I find my peace of mind?
Will this mind ever go to bed?
Will it ever stop with the insecurities and worries going on with my head?

Will I ever find the people who call me their home?
Will I ever be the person who doesn't care for a soul?
Will I ever be the person who doesn't hate herself?
Will I ever be the person who can sleep peacefully in the damn bed?

On the Edge

Have you ever had the urge to scream?
To be heard?
To be seen?
Well guess what that has been my whole life
The mom, dad, and the daughter who's just NICE.

I am the girl with a book in my hand
Wishing someone could understand
With no purpose or no aim
With a thousand internal demons to tame

I am the girl who is seventeen
The age to be keen
I have opinions, thoughts, and beliefs of my own
I am the girl whose faith is torn

I am the girl with peace on her face
And chaos, uncertainty, and hell on her mind.
But when asked if I'm okay, I say I'm fine.
So, I go to bed with a heavy heart and a fake smile
Wishing one day everything would be fine

Is Someone There?

Que Sera Sera...
Is what they say!
But I keep overthinking all day,
From which book I'm going to read
What outfit I'm going to wear?

I don't have a minute to spare
So, I breathe in, and I breathe out
But I am still full of doubts.
Have a lot to figure out
Trying to grow into a plant from a sprout.

An uncertain future and several panic attacks,
Leave me exhausted and I feel like a dejected sack.
Self confidence and self-esteem is what I lack,
Have a lot of emotional baggage to unpack.

The bottled feelings and unresolved fears,
Makes me feel inferior to my peers.
Only if they could see my tears...
I stay in solitude
Pretending to carry an attitude

The myriad advice, in my head reappears,
In the family gatherings and among my peers.
All seems unclear.

And I long for someone who could cheer!
And say 'I am always there...
One day everything would be clear.'

Shattered Reflections: The Struggle Within

I know you're disappointed
But it's your fault
Not mine!
After all you believed me when I said I was fine

Lost in life
Found in pages
I'm still trapped in my mental cages

Your parties and events
Filled me with that inevitable dread
To talk
To mingle
To explain why I'm still single

I don't know why I am this way
Why do I feel so exhausted every damn day?
Why do I even bother?
When everyone's here to play

I have no idea what to do
I just hate to bother you out of the blue

It's just it's never been this way
I've always known what to do when I wake up every single day

I had a plan
I had a road map
I was supposed to be on the stage
While the others clapped

Instead, I look in the mirror
And I stare at my mascara-streaked face
So yeah, I've been having a meltdown all this time
Glad you noticed, it's about time

I touch my cheek
To find the flicker of my nine-year-old self
She is still gathering dust at that cupboard shelf

I look her in the eye and ask-
"Still too afraid to ask for help?"
Oh lord what has become of me
Why do I want to always scream?

Maybe this is what rock bottom feels like
Always being exhausted
No matter how you've tried
To not be the person that I am
While no one even gives a single damn

With this realisation tears prickle my eyes
Is this what I get to feel for being nice?
Is this what I get to try to be poised and perfect?
That all my brain does is overthink and dissect

My tears flow through my cheeks
While my soul reeks
Of self-loathing and impending doom

I can't
I just can't do this anymore
Hide this pain that has been eating me whole

Always playing the smaller role
In this play that I call my life
It's true!
I'm a good for nothing child

Crying and pining over missed opportunities
Wondering about all the persons I can be
Just anything other than this weepy state
That I seem to have stuck since I was eight

Oh lord help me
For what I've become
Listening to every little insult
Makes me undone

Lord help me from this misery
I just want to be free
I just want to be free

Shadows of Self

Don't be so difficult
Come on, give me a smile
So, I did exactly that
I was just a child

I hate my nine-year-old self
Who started bottling up everything she felt
Anger, disappointment and pain
When she wanted a release
She started crying in the rain

I hate that she started practicing on how to talk
So that she wouldn't become the public's private laughing stock

I hate that she believed that dreams come true
That there won't be a single thing about herself she won't rue

I hate that she promised herself
No matter how much she grows up
There won't be a bridge between her and parents

There won't be any arguments
No slamming doors
No quest for being right

I hate that she looked a beat too long at the weighing scale
I hate that she started using the measuring tape
I hate that she started criticizing herself
God! I hate this pressure of loving oneself

I hate that she believed she will always know which way to go
Which decision to make
How much to grow

I hate that she believed she could be whatever she wanted
I hate that she believed that everything that she dreamed would eventually come true
Clearly, she had no idea that later she would be taunted

I hate that I wasn't a literal difficult child
Oh god
Why couldn't I have been rebellious?
Why couldn't I have been wild?
And why the hell I can't remove this plastered smile?

I hate that I always have been this civil
That putting on this mask of certainty has become a drill

In truth I have no idea why I carry this much hate
Why can't I have a minute to stop?
Why can't I let this mask drop?
Why can I be so easily told and tamed?
I guess I have no one else but me to blame

Silent Screams

Where do you go when your house isn't your home?
Do you run away?
Or do you stick for the show?

The tension
The drama
The fear
The pain
I can list a thousand reasons for your pain
It won't change the way you live
It won't relax your shoulders, so stiff

The point is you drift apart
From your body
From your heart
When someone asks - "What the hell is wrong with you!?"
You don't know where to start

But nothing compares to your dramatic family dinners
There are only losers, no winners
In this competition to be mean
Yup, you got it right, they also work in teams

They start with asking about your weight
Then they judge you by the content of your plate
They whisper
They gossip in hushed tones

Then they move to your attire
They look at your crop top as if it's on fire
They talk about wearing 'appropriate clothes ' that are conservative and right
And not so subtle way, they tell you that you need to diet

Then they ask about your ex
If he's the reason you bought that backless dress

They eye you as a bomb that needs to be diffused
Like a problem that needs to be solved
Like a dog that needs to be muzzled
Like trash that can't even be re used

You walk away
Because you can't take it anymore
You return to your corner of the room
You start to overthink your impending doom

Your dad jokes 'Our little girl's so quiet. Sometimes we forget that she even exists!"
His audience laughs
Oblivious to the typical father- daughter drift

Then you're mom's next
She starts to compliment your already perfect cousin sister
She gushes over her lost weight
But she wasn't the one who's been trying to impress her, since she was eight
Well, this mother- daughter relationship is already doomed
It's already too late

You play your part
You play your role
You become a wall
You resist the urge to crawl

They ask you about school
When they're just being cruel
They ask about the two friends you have
They ask if they are really interested in being your friend, or are they still trapped

Then they ask if you can really talk
Or are you just a robot that your parents bought
Your parents laugh at the painful jibe
After all they are all part of this tribe

You wonder how many of them would care
If you matched their stares
Their disapproving scowls
Their natural ability to put someone down

You smile and you nod at the right places
You suppress and bury any kind of hurt or even its traces
So that you remain in their good graces

You laugh at their hurtful quips and jokes
You resist the urge to choke
Sometimes you wish that you have a stroke
So that they release how much you have they really broke

How much of you is taint and saint
They praise how good are you trained
Since you endured every hurtful comment and jibe

You never once cried
You guess a part of you died
You never once screamed
Be real, this is reality, no dream

So, I guess I must come back to the question that's been haunting my mind
Where do you go when your house isn't your home?
Do you ever leave?
Or do you still live there?
Where, just parts of you are gradually still dying

I Love Being a Woman!

I love being a woman
No, I genuinely do!

I love that there is comfortable silence amongst us
I love that we stick together
When life feels blue

I love that we cry together
I love that cheer for each other
Whenever we win

I love that we share frowns together
I love our secret grins
I love that we stick for each other through thick and thin

I love our secret book club
Where we pine over mysterious fictional men
I love it when we judge them out of ten

I love that we scream Taylor Swift lyrics on the top of our lungs
We dance
We twirl
We create our own little world

I love it when we go to overpriced cafes and bars
I love that we are old school
I love that we all still look at the stars
I love that we all cried to 'The Notebook'

I love that we all have that one show that got us completely hooked
I love that we have that one celebrity crush
Whose one look has melted our temperament, so rough

I know being a woman is also tough
You must straighten your shoulders and keep your chin up
But it's also nice to see all these women dressed in pink
Watching 'Barbie' and being cringe

I love that we have the freedom to dream
I love that girlhood is so clean
Full of loyalty and warmth
Even though we have our own lives with our boundaries drawn

I love that we still pout
That we hype up each other
Kicking the self-doubt out

We help each other shine
We're like a tribe
We hug and we dance
We have our own stance

I love that we have a secret language
I love that a single nod can hold so much meaning
I love that we convince each other that one bad day
means we're just dreaming

I love our chaotic and messy selves
One day we'll have a whole shelf
Of memories
Of love
Of bonds
Proof that when you take care of things nothing can go
wrong

Unspoken Longing

There she goes
She does it again
Hurts me in a way that no one can

There was a time when we were inseparable
And now it's her that I can't stand

She over gives and over cares
And when I look out for myself, she just stares
With strong criticism and a balanced smile
She compares me to her niece who she considers a rare sapphire

She treats her like a perfect queen
And me like a messy and dirty room that needs to be cleaned
She gives her the love that I never received
And every time she compares us
I feel like I've been deceived

She considers her as the daughter
She already has
Pretty, soft spoken, Girly, obedient and kind
She believes her to be one of her kind

But what about me?
I want to scream
I wish that it's just a bad dream

What about the moments that we had?
Before life became so sad
Before we drifted apart
I am talking about the hospital room
Where everything starts

What happened to us?
How did our relationship become so rocky and rough?
Is it something I did?
I was just a kid

"Sit properly Dorothea"
"Cross your legs"
"Look at your sister, she's so perfect and well kept"
Your voice keeps ringing in my head
I'm sure I will keep hearing it
even when I am dead

You raised me
You've bred me
You've taught me everything I know
So how can you say that I am incapable of growth?

I just feel exhausted all the time
It feels like my existence is like a crime

Am I past my prime?
With this knowledge I cried

Oh, please tell me what have I not done?
I've listened and implemented everything you've said
Tell me more about how I can fill your eyes with pride!?
Tell me! Goddamnit!
I'll do it anyway

No matter how much it makes me grey
No matter how much of me dies
At least I can say that I tried
To be the perfect girl you've always wanted
Maybe I will even forget the way you've always haunted
my mind
If I become this version of me
Will I finally earn a word from that is kind?

Will I finally earn your love?
Will I finally transform from an ugly duckling to a
beautiful swan?
Will you finally love me the way I deserve?
Will this hole you created in my heart never hurt?

Struggle Behind Surface

I am tired of pretending that I like the way I am
I am exhausted of pretending that I don't give a damn
I am tired of the people that surround me
They are the ones who constantly drown me

Their questions
Their stares
Their prayers
"Oh, lord, please help this girl!"
For I am not their precious little girl anymore
When I breakdown and lay on the floor

I am tired of being the thorn in this bed of roses
I am tired of being the ugly duckling to their swan
I don't want to be me anymore from dusk to dawn

They look at me with judgement mixed with concern
They call the doctor
For I am unwell
For I am untested
Thus, no way to be trusted

Frustration doesn't begin to describe how I feel
When I watch my everyone reel

When I watch how they deal
This disease that I have
Oh, I'm sorry for not being grateful. My bad!

Then the audience starts to gather
They gasp in shock and surprise
I explain to them that I tried to be sane
But they all eye me with disdain

Friends, family and all the people that I knew
Started leaving me as restless as I grew
So, I scream - "It's not fair!"
And tear off a chunk of my hair
Because, why not, it's not like anyone cares

They forget every moment that we had
Everything we did
Now they don't even sit near me
I guess, that's the result of letting your emotions free

They don't know what I've been through
They don't know that this pain will help me grow
Or maybe I'll finally become that thing worthy to be thrown

They forget about the little girl in pigtails
The girl who believed in stories and tales
They just gawk and murmur how her life went off rails

They don't talk about her love for books
How can they?
When they've been busy searching for flaws and crooks
That's all they take from the girl they've known, since she was eight

They assess and analyse
Her body, her size
Meanwhile ignoring all her sighs and cries for help
They never cared, no matter how alone she felt

They never cared about how broken and bruised she felt
They assess her as a problem to be dealt
I guess that's what I get for being anything other than stealth

What I want?
What I want is to be held
To be told that I am going to okay,
Even if they have no proof, no say
In the future ahead
I just want someone to hold me and wipe my unshed tears in bed

Yearning for Yesterday?

I just want to be loved without being shredded to pieces
I want people to stay
At least more than a single day

I want to go back to my childhood
I want to undo everything I've done wrong
I want to remember that song
That I used to sing at the top of my lungs
While ignoring judgemental stares who clearly had no idea what was fun

I want to go back to that Ice cream shop
The one where me and my siblings go
We would press our faces on the display glass in awe
With our jaws dropped

I want to go back to that first scholastic fair
Where I first fell in love with books
With my hand intertwined with my mom's hand
Walking through the isles
We both looked at the bookshelves with the curiosity of a newborn child

I want to go back to that plastic tent
That me and my siblings used to assemble
Because not even the skyscrapers can resemble
To the memories
To the laughter
To the innocence of summer days
When life was all about ice cream flavours and sunny days

I want to go back to my childhood home
A sanctuary of peace and hope oblivious to the impending chaos

I want to go back to my childhood self
I want to undo all the damage she did to herself
I want to shake her by the shoulders
I want to mend her
I want to fix her
I want to change her into someone that fits in

But I won't give her any false hope
That finally her family peeks behind her stoic mask
That making friends won't be such a task
That your personality becomes sun basked
That you finally realised that you need help, and guess what! You asked!

I want to go back to my late grandfather
I want to stop him from dying

Or maybe I would just do some crying
I would ask why I am such a loser, even though I am trying!

I want to go back and save that guy
I want to tell him that life is much more beautiful than it seems
Or maybe I'll ask him to take me with him
At least that would solve the problem of everyone calling me out about me being so grim

I want to go back to save my little sister
I want to just get her to live!
Or maybe I'll just hug her tight
I'll tell her that I would miss her
But I'll eventually be alright
I would tell her that I love her
That I miss her everyday
Every damn time when I eat french fries on a bad day

I just want to go back to my mom and dad
I just want to hug them both
I want to hear them call me their 'precious girl' until they don't
I want to warn them that I am going to let them down
That I won't ask them for their help in the future, even when I drown
I'll tell them that we drift apart
At least they'll get a head start

I want to go back to childhood self
I want to watch myself laugh
Before my life fell apart
Before anxiety knocked on the door
The fear that my company will only bore
Before the grief sneaked in
Before people around me had this obsession to see me thin

Before I became this broken and bruised version of me
When all I did was stay under the tree
With a Jane Austen novel in my hand
With my imagination and optimism high
When I never had to muffle my screams and cries
When I was appreciated when I tried
When the parts of me were still alive that slowly and
gradually died

Unraveled

I hate you for what you did
And I miss you like a little kid
I don't know which emotion to focus on
The anger, longing or the love that's long gone

We aren't what we used to be
The family of make believe
We stopped being a family a long time ago
We just had to, to grow

As I grew, I related to Matilda a lot
The feeling of loneliness
The constant pain in the chest
The permanent parasite of distraught

You played a big role in this pain
I didn't know whether to let go or carry this emotional bullshit.
This thought alone was enough to send me through fits

You only saw me when I fit
In the mould created by you

It didn't matter that my soul was black and blue
I kicked myself up and passed through every of your hoops

Like a circus animal
I was chained
I was drained
I was trained
To put on a show

To stay put, nod and smile at the appropriate times
I wanted to be perfect to you
But I was oblivious to the signs

Signs of hidden games were always there
In their whispers
In their stares
Their hushed tones
I started to faze under their gaze

Anxiety choked me
Pushed me around
I could never find a stable ground
I started looking for my past self in lost and found

Their presence drowned me deep
I started to observe them from afar
Like some deranged creep

I needed to find out before they pulled me inside with them in the deep

I took out my red round wagon
It was my personal dragon
I took my clothes, some snacks, and books

I felt like Matilda that day
To break free of so-called family
To wake up to a new day
To finally be able to distinguish between black, white, and grey

I just wanted to walk the right way, what can I say?
I guess I got played
By one of your games
Now you won't take blame
Of trouble you caused
We locked eyes and the moment just passed
As our relationship lies here, tossed.

Nothing can be done to undone whatever had been done
Whatever had been said
So now here I lie
With the knowledge that you are gone officially from this world
With our relationship long lost and burned

Nightmarish Ninteenth

Tears cascade over my cheeks
Mascara smudged under my eyes
I try to muffle my sobs and sighs

It's my nineteenth birthday in a week
Hence the tears-streaked cheeks
My anxiety peaks at night
When I try to imagine my future but see nothing in sight

I don't want to celebrate it, you know
I mean what's the use
When I've experienced negligible growth
What would happen if I ever choked?

I hate birthdays
And it's a fact
Because no one in the room stays
For the lowest version of me
One the sight of the first crack, they flee

My sobs grow violent
But the house stays silent

My mum and dad have no clue
About the broken pieces of me I've tried to piece together through glue

My soul back and blue
Can't take this anymore
The fake promises and smiles
I wonder where my innocence went.
I guess time really flies!

I hate when people say that they are grateful that I was born
As if I'm a rose instead of a thorn
Like they would care
If they find me gone

I hate wearing new clothes
I hate wearing a fake smile
When all I want to do
Is lay on the floor and die

So, I settle for crying
Since I have not been granted the privilege of dying
I stuff a fist against my mouth
Because in a room full of suns no one needs a cloud

I cry for the girl I was
I cry for the innocence that I've lost
I cry because I had a childhood that couldn't be paused

I cry for the present me
Who's so depressed inside out
That all I feel is self-doubt

I cry the person I'll never be
The girl who could laugh
The girl who wasn't afraid to try
The girl who could scream and shout to the sky
She couldn't give any justifications as to why

I cry and I cry
Until my voice dies down
Until my face is all red
Until someone rises from their bed

I wipe my tears
I try to be happy to be nineteen
But all I want to do is scream at myself
"What's wrong with you, you freak? !!"

But I don't
Since It's my birthday
And I have a role
To be grateful and smile

I must look at the cake that has 'Happy Nineteenth '
inscribed
I must celebrate my birthday
When most of me have already died

But I guess I will pretend to be happy once a year
Because all these people in this room will steer clear
Of the girl that I am
The girl who is bitter and dry
The girl who can't speak
The girl who's a freak
So, I guess this is goodbye to the version of these people who are probably high
But the effect won't last long
Because no one stays and -
Oh, look they've already gone!

Oh Lily!

I have a question for you, Lily
Why did you stop being silly?
Why did you become serious of all sudden?
Come on, you're already a burden

Oh Lily,
You were the funniest little kid
You always greeted everyone with a joke
Don't you remember?
What do you mean by that you barely even spoke?

Oh Lily
You were our perfect little angel
You were so well mannered
Don't lie to us!
By telling you were hurting inside
That you felt that you had no one to confide

Oh Lily
You were our perfect kid
What do you mean?
You want to stay by yourself in your room?

Oh Lily
You never had a bad temper
You never threw unnecessary tantrums at us
So, what changed between us?

Oh Lily
You were thin as a paper
You wanted to be tall as a skyscraper
So why did you stop standing on the weighing scale?
What do you mean that you fear what it will show?
How dare you talk to us about your growth!

Oh Lily
You were so polished
You were so poised
What do you mean?
That we used you like a toy

Oh Lily
You were incomparable in our eyes
Don't you dare bitch and moan about how we compared
you with your older sister
Maybe we wouldn't have
If you had been even more thin, beautiful, and poised

Oh Lily
Why did you throw all your Barbie dolls away?
What do you mean by you don't want them to stay!?

Oh Lily
My little one
Don't be so dumb
What do you mean by you need freedom and space?
Talk to us when you can appreciate your own face

Oh Lily
Stop reading instantly at once
Stop being so abnormal
Come on, do something fun
For once

Oh Lily
Who said that you can wear this mini skirt?
Stop it!
Stop feeling so hurt!
Don't be so absurd!

Oh Lily
Why do you write so bitter about us
Remember you'll always love us
What do you mean by being a part of one of us is tough?

Oh Lily
Don't you dare change!
Don't you express your rage!
Don't you feel so much at once!
Look at you!
You don't even have the nerve to confront!

Oh Lily
This cage has forever been your home
What do you mean by you want to leave?
We've given you so much
We've sacrificed too much
To let go of you

You'll stay!
Do you hear me!??
Even if your soul becomes black and blue
Even if you feel of no use
Even if you feel broken and bruised

You'll stay here!
Be our perfect little girl!
Come on,
You owe us!
Especially after what you've said and done

One Day

One day I'm going to live in a house of my own
One day I'll have everything that I want

One day it would all make sense
Every meltdown
Every high point
Every descent

One day I won't feel so hopeless anymore
I would finally convince people that I've got some talent in store

One day I'll prove her wrong
Every girl who's pushed me around
One day they'll see
What I've been building
While they were busy throwing belittling catch phrases

One day I'll make them proud
My mum and my dad and the nine-year-old me
One day I'll give them reasons for being happy

One day I won't be so bitter anymore
I'll give people good days and more

Maybe I'll finally meet someone
Maybe I would even become fun

One day I'll tell them that I have always had a lot to say
But maybe I would have said them
If any single one of them had stayed

One day I will be taken seriously
Not some girl they played
With their not-so-subtle jabs
Their not so gentle quips
I hope some of them die in a blip

Anyway, one day I might get a tattoo
Somewhere hidden
But something meaningful
That only speaks my truth

One day I'll have a cat
Maybe two
Maybe three
Anyway, we'll be a family

One day I'll have a stable life
I'll have a career
Maybe then people won't steer clear of that version of me
They'll promise
They'll stay

One day I'll have everything that I desire
Maybe while talking to people, I won't perspire

One day I'll be invited to places
Maybe they'll see me more than my friendly face
They'll understand the things unsaid
Or maybe it will go over their heads

One day this will all make sense
These black and blue days
These impending amends
The constant need to bend
To other's rules and trends
The absence of any friends

Maybe one day, I'll find myself
Hanging out by the fiction isle
At local bookstore in the end
Surrounded by books
My Constants
My best friends

Weaving Dreams Into Reality

If I were a character in a book
Everything that I do and say would make sense
It would have a beginning, middle and an end

If I were a character in a book
I would be the character who stays in the corner of the room
I would be the one forgotten too soon

I would be observing all the people in the room
I would pay attention to their steps
The way they laugh
The way they talk
I guess you could say that I stalk

I would wonder why I can't be more like them.
That's when I slam into someone's chest
A beautiful stranger whose gaze feels like a caress

I would try not to blush but will eventually fail
Because it's me of course
He would take in my magnificent red gown
He'll make his life mission to permanently remove my frown

His smiling eyes would connect with my sad ones
His gaze would comfort me as much as my F.R.I.E.N.D.S re runs

He would smile
I would smile
This will go on for a while
I would wonder why the hell am I behaving like a child?

He would lean closer
I would be covered with all of him
His cologne reminding me of sugar cookies and cinnamon buns

We would talk in hushed tones
We would promise each other letters instead of phones

We would laugh
We would flirt
Maybe I'll feel brave enough to wear a skirt

Eventually we would part
With happiness and love in our hearts
We would promise to meet again through our eyes
With this we would exchange our goodbyes

I would blush
I would swoon
There would be a big spotless moon

I would wear a light pink floral gown
I would be the talk of the town
I would listen to my heart, instead of my head
Here I would sleep in my bed

I would listen to good music
Read good fables
I would finally live a life, which is stable

I would drink healing tea
I would be free
Of all problems
And past
I won't live through life, I will dance!

I would have this cottage up the hill
Covered in ivy
Where time would stand still

There I would write fables
That would be the safe space for Mable
Sitting in the middle row
But yet to be seen
She'll always have my fables to keep her company

But Alas I would have to come back to real life
Where I'll have to work a boring job from nine to five
I'll have to deal with insecurities
And boring snobs!

I'll build a home
With love!
With warmth!
With laughter!
And books!
Lots and Lots of books!

We Are Women!

We are women
We lose our identity
We find them again
All the while going through period cramp pain

We are women
We gain
We lose
We can have a successful career and a successful marriage
Why do we have to choose?

Some of us still wear glitter
Some of us have turned bitter
But no matter who we are
We all hide our scars

Some of us smile in pain
Some of us lash out in the worst possible way
Some of us are more vocal about the pain we go through
Some of us silently grew

Being a woman is not easy in this world
So, we hold hands and make it tolerable
It's ok, we are allowed to be vulnerable

We constantly re-invent ourselves
We refuse to be used as an artifact on a shelf
But we also aren't too ashamed to ask for help

Whether it's wearing pink to Barbie movie
Or wearing friendship bracelets at Taylor Swift concert
Our childhood returned
It felt like fresh air after being so much burned

We are born in this world
With a purpose
With an aim
Sometimes even if you lose
You still enjoy the game

Remember, girls?
When we all chipped in to buy that Barbie dollhouse
The one that was pink
But disappeared from our lives in a blink

Remember our awe over stupid glitter pens
The constant urge to follow different trends
The little group of people in school we all called friends
Who turned out to be snakes
So, you mind your own business and eat your own
birthday cake

Being a happy woman in this world is hard
But I guess you could always start

Maybe tomorrow
Maybe today
Maybe you could at least try once a day

They laugh on the top of their lungs
While making terrible 'strict wife jokes'
Or delivering taunts
About our driving
The way of our surviving
They all hate when they see a woman thriving

So, hold hands and just feel
Because every woman has a different way to deal
With grief
With life
With annoying neighbour
Poor souls are mentally deprived!

Being a woman is not all that bad
It's just sad
To be underestimated and misunderstood all the time
To hide our pain but still pretend to be fine
Is being a happy woman in this world such a crime?

This Gnawing Grief

I've been miserable
No one even knows
I guess I do put up a good show

I've been feeling like this as long as I can remember
But to be accurate, last December
It's when grief knocked on my door
When everyone slept
I would break down on the floor

I can still see you now
Your curly hair
Your sunny disposition
Your warm smile
It's like you're still here, alive

I have tried to forget that you don't exist anymore
That's what I tell myself to get myself off the floor
But in the end, it's not true
Leaving me reeling
My soul black and blue

Some people just leave
Without saying any word
And it hurts

I'm sorry I couldn't be there in the funeral
Sorry that I couldn't say my last goodbye
Sorry that last time that we saw each other
I couldn't even say hi

So, I send flowers to your mom
She sounds tired and broken on the phone
I guess it's tough to bury the one you gave birth
The weight of your grief can shatter the Earth

I wrote letters to you
That I couldn't send
I wrote poems about you
To go through
This difficult period of pain
Where I've been surviving, barely sane

I tried to call you to hear a voice
I tried not to cry when I heard it in an old video of ours
Can you hear my muffled sobs in the stars?

I tried to stop my tears
But I failed
No one noticed

Not even my peers
When the news related to your death came to me clear

My mom broke down in the middle of the street
My world collapsed three feet deep
When I heard you were already gone
How could I see someone get buried
Who I saw as a newborn?

There was a sadness in the air
I don't know why
But I kept picturing your hair in my head
Maybe it distracted me from my internal pit of dread

I kept wondering what would have happened
If you had lived?
Would you have been an annoying teen?
Would you have found the thing that you loved?
Would you have had experiences of your own?
I would have loved to see you grown

So, tell me,
Did it hurt when you died?
Did it hurt that we couldn't say goodbye?
I have all these questions in my head
But I don't have you
And with that realization
I begin my daily routine of crying in my bed

Beneath the Surface

It's okay that you left
Leaving them bereft and reeling
Walking out is the first step of healing

I know that you miss them like a kid
Even though you hate them for what they did
Honey, there's tears clinging to your eyelashes
As memories flash in your mind in flashes

Happy memories
Sad memories
Memories that you wished you buried in your mind
The unknown dark side

I know you feel bad
For not feeling sad
About leaving the place that was supposedly your home
But you remember those memories that are set in stone

Isn't it strange?
That you can miss the people who've hurt you
Once
Twice

Thrice
You live together as a family
But at what price?

It's like playing a character in a play
Some get killed
Some get to stay
Some were barely there

You had to play the role
You really had to live the role
Each day
You had to be someone you're not
Then slowly and gradually you see yourself distort

Each role had to be played with great precision
You will overthink your every decision
Your every choice
But it won't muffle the noise

The noise in your head will grow louder each day
You will experience severe chest pain
You'll cry with the rain
And somehow it will lessen the pain for a brief period of time
Until it increases with no advance signs

You'll blame yourself for their actions
You'll fill your plates in fractions

They will contract your self esteem
You'll second guess everything you believe

There will be days when you will feel relieved
There will be days when you'll feel stressed
But mostly you'll be depressed

There will be situations that will be out of your control
They will take over the emotional toll
Over you
Over everyone
But at the end of the day, you'll be blamed
After everything is said and done

So how do you leave a place like this?
Such a place which always pretends to be bliss
But that place was hurting you inside
So, you find a place to hide

So hide
From the people you please
From the anxious screaming
From the constant daydreaming
From your nine-year-old self
Who's constantly screaming for help

Façade of Smiles

Am I not enough?
She asks herself with tears clouding her eyes
She looks at herself in the mirror
She doesn't like what she sees
Well, that's not a surprise!

She wears her pearl tops
To try to save a film
That's already a flop
Maybe if things go wrong
She can become Cinderella and flee the party at the pin drop

She sighs but complies with her my mother's demands
Mostly to avoid any reprimands
And enters the hustle bustle of the party
With a polite smile
She feels she's living in the world of men
Where she's still a child

She politely nods
At all the frauds
Filled in the room
Everyone's here with their personal boon

They laugh
They flirt
Their personality is probably not even worth the dirt

Soon she addresses them all
Ignoring their heights so tall
They respond with analysing stares
Which makes her feel as if she's standing in the party, naked and bare

But she remains perfectly still
Until their egos have been fulfilled
Then she takes a step back
Mostly to avoid herself from falling on the floor like a sack
Or to hide the cracks

She takes a drink
But she can still feel their judgemental stares
Analysing her
Judging her
Criticizing her
Every detail
Every little thing about her that fails

So, she eventually goes to the corner of the room
Where she stares back at them
The only place where she feels advantage over them

Here she can observe their strength and weakness
The cracks in their finesse
Their emotions successfully suppressed
Everyone in this room smiles and laughs
When they're all depressed

She feels sorry for these people
She feels sorry for herself
She really hates the rules of society
That everyone seems so afraid to bend

She, then fetches herself too much food
She doesn't care if she's being called 'rude'
She really doesn't care for an opinion by some dude

She chomps on cheese and bread
She sits at the dining table with dread
She smiles at the people who call themselves her allies
When they're all spies!

Well, eventually the party ends
Everyone leaves
Later she descends
On her comfortable bed
With her constant companion, dread

Embracing Life's Story

At some point, you're going to have to turn the page.
You're going to age
Like wine
Or like that yellow crinkled page

You'll lose
You'll gain
You'll get used to the pain

There will be good days and bad
One day you'll allow yourself to be sad
You'll make mistakes
But don't worry, you won't become your dad

I know you feel that you're still that kid
Who's told to be quiet and sit
I know you don't feel any growth
You sometimes wish to have a stroke

You'll love
And you'll break
You'll take risks
Irrespective of the high stakes

You'll have a home of your own
You'll live and love alone
Because by then everyone you know will be gone

They will go to their lives
Where they would take their words, they use as knives
But they'll still mock you
And laugh at every baby step you take
And call you fake
While you alone break

You'll gain some knowledge about the world
You'll know some things are just experienced not taught
But by the end of it all you'll be left distraught

You'll experience grief
And it's visit won't be brief
You will handle it in your own way
Each day will feel like another horrible day

You'll try new things
But quickly face the challenges life brings
Sometimes the introvert is forced to sing
You'll meet people made of different strings

But life's not all bad
I guess you do feel sad
About not figuring out who you are

Whether you're going to be successful
Or happy
Or just keep burning like a star

You will make decisions
You will chase after precision
In your work
In yourself
God, you'll miss the days when you believed in Santa and his elves

Maybe you'll become bitter
Maybe you'll lose everything you own
You'll feel hopeless
You'll feel stressed
You'll feel depressed
Maybe you won't like to look at yourself when you undress

You'll grow your hair longer
Or maybe cut it short
Maybe you'll try to convince yourself
That you don't need help

But time changes
It ranges
From good to bad
From bad to good

Life's a combination of your good and bad decision
It never demands precision
Yes, decisions are to be made
Sometimes you are going to feel like you're going to fade

But hey!
Life gives new chances every day
You meet people and challenges for an aim
Then slowly and gradually
You'll turn into a person they can't tame
You'll have everything that you want

You will be invited to places
Where you will be admired by countless faces
Or maybe you'll be a mystery to the world
Who just crashed and burned but never returned

Happy Birthday?

I am turning nineteen this week
And I wonder what difference it would make.
If I change my age
Will I let myself out of my mental cage?

I'll still have the same insecurities
Will I have any different priorities?
I'll still have the same flaws, if not more
My mood swings will still be a seesaw

Will the change in the last digit
Change my status of being insipid?
Will it change my demeanor so rigid?
Will it end my desire to fit?

Is growing up supposed to be this hard?
Is having a day of peace barred?
Why is womanhood so sad?
Why do I make everyone's day bad?

Is it normal?
Or is it just me?
That thinks birthdays are depressing as hell

Like it puts you under how much you haven't achieved spell
Tell me that's what you all feel
Maybe there's a way I can heal

A birthday cake will be cut
Candles will be blown
The birthday song will be sung
But it won't over power the self-deprecating inner voice
But it won't change the fact that you'll always be the
second choice

They say we celebrate birthdays to celebrate someone's
birth
But I keep repeating 'The Road not taken' excerpt
I can't just forget all the hurt

Once I was a newborn
Innocent and adored
Maybe already a bit bored

Then I was six
When my mom gave me the loneliness quick fix
She introduced me to reading
Books felt freeing
I read books like breathing

Then I was thirteen
I was happy
Oblivious to the future bad dreams

Then I became seventeen
Then started -
Daily nightmares
Judgemental stares
The inability of being vulnerable and bare

Then came eighteen
Everything's going to be fine, right?
After all I'm an adult
But we don't always get our desired result

Anyway, I am turning nineteen in a week
Have lost a lot
Have gained a lot
Have learnt a little
You can say I've gotten a bit bitter

So, what do you say?
What exact difference does my birthday make?
If I'm going to live in the same sad mental state
How to live a life?
When life never even gives a break

Dreams Amidst Despair

Another night
Another breakdown
Another day of wishing I was an alcoholic
So that I had some alcohol to drown

To drown
Worries
Pain
Grief
All these emotions knock my door
But their visit is never brief

I stare at the ceiling
Because for some reason that seems appealing

I guess I am just reeling
From all the events that I experienced when I was eighteen
I released my pain in the form of silent tears and muffled screams

Why don't parents tell their child that not every one of their dreams come true?
That they'll rue waking up every day

That no miracle can stop your downfall
No matter how much you pray

I toss and turn in my bed
I overthink the way I can keep my family fed
Then I decided to focus on creating my new book couple playlist instead

I turn to look in the window
I picture people sleeping in their beds
Oblivious to other people's silent breakdowns
To their muffled screams
To their nightmares that they forget about next day like normal dreams

I turn to the other side to find my brother asleep
I wonder what he dreams about
A plant that I have been seeing growing from a sprout
Will this little guy also suffer from self-doubt?

I finally give up and go back to the ceiling
It's pitch black
It's nothing but me
And my bottled-up feelings

I think about death
I think about grief
I think that all good moments in life feels so brief

I sometimes wish for a soulmate
But I guess then I'll have to believe in faith
Never mind, I'm being delusional
Distracting myself from my sad state

I think maybe one day I'll be a bestselling author
I'll go on book tours
I'll have millions of readers
That I'll live my dreams for sure

I'll grin like an idiot
I'll make scenarios in my head
I'll write everything in my notes app
Especially the things best left unsaid

Finally sleep finds my way
I'll try to keep my eyes open
To write poems about all the things they say that leave my heart broken

That Unspoken Goodbye

This grief that I carry in my heart
Has started to tear apart
My soul black and blue

Hurt fills my chest
As I see another loved one being put to rest
They say - 'May she rest in peace'
I hope she can still leave her last piece

Every laughter
Every cry
I remember it all without any effort of trying

Memories flood my mind
I'm trying to find every piece of her
I can find

I remember her kind laugh
I remember her warm smile
I genuinely try to smile

I feel numb to the bone
I even forgot what's supposed to be my role

I sit like a sack on a chair
I don't care how I look
Yup, even if I got greasy hair

My heart breaks for the grieving mom and dad
I can't even imagine what's on their mind
How would I know?
How can one imagine the pain of losing their child?

My heart breaks for their little brother
Who has no idea what's going on
He just missed the sister that's forever gone

I look at her favourite teddy bears
I look at the broken version of people who are usually the source of judgemental stares
Now they are all remembering her in their prayers

She loved eating French fries
Did you know?
My heart breaks with the knowledge that she didn't get a chance to grow

I try not to think too much when I eat french fries
Because I see her widened eyes
Waiting in anticipation
As if French fries were the greatest creation

I often wonder what would have happened
If she had lived
If she was still here
With her curly hair
And warm smile
Maybe everything would have been fine

But she's gone
To a place from where she can't come back
Leaving cracks
In our heart
How am I going to move on?
How am I going to even start?

Silent Turmoil

Missed my breakfast again
When someone asks me if I'm okay.
I guess I'll just pretend
To be fine
Maybe even slap on a smile.

I get up from my bed
With the intention of getting to the bread
All the while my mental health is hanging by a thread.

I look at the sky
I wonder if it remembers
How much I cried
The previous night
When there was no sunlight in sight

I look at the park
And see children laughing and playing
This reminds of the time I thought everyone was staying

Anyway
So, I go to the shower
And try to forget

Every problem
Every distress
I wonder if my favourite top is pressed

I look at my complete manuscript
Wondering if it's worth something
Or maybe it's just shit

I wonder if this is THE moment
Or maybe it's just a miss
Oh, look another person looks at me, equally pissed.

I try to focus on work
I try not to think about it
I try not to overthink about it
Yet again I fail
I would give anything to see what my future entails

I wonder if my work will hurt the people I love
Will they see me differently?
Now that they know what I think of them
Will that greet me in public?
Or upon my sight, hide in their den?

I run my hand across my face
I wonder if I'll ever be okay
Will I ever have a peaceful day?

A day with no noise in my head
When I can sleep in my bed
When I won't analyse and overthink
Everyone's every move, every sigh
When I won't have panic attacks
Which makes me feel like I'm going to die

I don't know what the future holds
At least that's what the therapist said
I wonder if there are any loop holes in what she said

I wonder if anyone will find out the books I read
I wonder if I'll ever get to live my dreams
I wonder if what I write is trash.

Maybe I'm just being too rash
To my family
To myself
Maybe I'm hurting myself
Instead of asking for actual help?

Stargazing

I've always wondered what it would be like
To reside amongst the stars
Would we still feel lonely?
Even after going so far?

When we reach the sky
Are we going to remember that guy?
Who broke up with us through text
And we went through the biggest breakup of our lives
without any context

When we reach the sky
Are we still going to strive to be the best?
Are we going to analyse our past life's tests?
Are we still going to judge and analyse our flaws?
Are we still going to burn ourselves from dusk to dawn?

When we reach the sky
Are we still going to hide our cracks?
Are we still going to experience silent panic attacks?

Are we still going to act less emotionally?
Like it's a fact

Are we still going to self-depreciate for not being able to act?
To act normal around the people who surround us
To the people who intentionally drown us

Are we going to remember that weighing scale?
Who used to be the judge
Of whether we'll be called a matchstick or a big whale

Are we still going to search for happiness in this material world?
Or are we going to shine by ourselves?
Even though we would burn

They say when we die, we become a star
Will this mean that we would meet the people that we've lost?
The people who we miss everyday of our lives
Our memories together stab through my mind like sharp knives

But I have a question for every person there present in the sky
Is it worth being present there every night?
While the loved ones you left here are desperate for your one last sight

What goes on your mind?
When lovers count you on their first date night

Do you laugh at them?
Or do you play along?
Can you sense when two people together feel wrong?

Can you hear people weeping?
Can you hear their muffled sobs and cries?
When they shift their tears clouded eyes towards the sky
Do you look them in the eye?
Do you have answers?
When they ask in an anguished tone, "Why?"

Can you hear their pain?
Do you feel protective of them?
When people call them insane

Oh Stars!
You really reside so far
But you serve as an idea for a date
You hear us question our own fate
You see every one of us shed emotions
You hear us screaming and crying to you about our mind's constant commotion

You really are something
Don't you know?
You've seen us lost
You've seen us grow
You've seen good people get what they deserve and even more

The End of Us

I read your message
My stomach dropped
You called me
But I let the phone ring
I didn't want to experience the pain your voice brings

A sudden flash of memories played in my mind
Our first meeting
The first time we talked
Our first fight
The moment I realised that our friendship wasn't right

I sighed as I remember these past few months
Everything that was said and done
Every time you left
Then you came back again
As if your absence hadn't caused any pain

We were good together
Once upon a time
We used to sing songs
We used to believe that our bond was strong

We used to giggle and grin
In the classroom
In the ground
With you, a smile replaced my frowns

But sometimes people aren't what they show
It's a matter of time before they show their true side
And you realise the person you once knew has long died

I confided in you
I almost became a child with you
But somehow, after all this time
It feels that you never grew

You shit talked behind my back
You called me mean, weak and sad
At least you were honest with someone
I'll give you that

You targeted me time and time again
But then you apologized with your sweet and heartfelt texts
I could feel something wrong in my chest

You brushed everything under the rug
And left at the slightest disagreement
You accused me of being a bad friend
I knew it was the beginning of the end

You left again
I realised
You had changed
But so had I
So, this time I didn't call your name
Because I was sick and tired of your games

I realised that I don't want to pass your tests
I told myself it's time to part ways
It was for the best

However, as I stared at the ceiling
I was reeling
From the text from you on my birthday
As if it was yet another day

Tears clouded my eyes
As I left you on seen
And rejected your call

I was angry
I was annoyed
That all I've been to you was a toy

I grieved
The bond that we shared
The secrets that we bared
The songs that we used to sing
Now every memory of you stings

They say friendship breakups hurt the most
I agree
But I will admit
I feel free
Of games
Of a forced friendship
Of constantly begging you to stay and solve
I feel liberated and strong
Now that our friendship has dissolved.

In the Silences of 4 AM

It's four a.m.
But I still don't want to sleep
I want answers
To the questions that are playing in my mind on repeat

I don't know why
But I keep bursting into tears
I blame my fears
And the lack of technology to see our future
crystal clear

I hate that the only thing I'm good at
is not given the importance it deserves
And it hurts so damn much
I guess life really is tough

I re read my manuscript for the thousandth time
I wonder if these words will be printed on pages
I wonder will anyone connect to these phrases

I wonder if they'll even read what I have to say
I wonder if they'll like what I write
Something that has been a product of many sleepless
nights

I toss and turn
My stomach churns
As I await an email

An email that states that they like what I write
That they see some potential in what they read
That they would give me a chance
To start living my dream as soon as I can

But alas!
There is no email stating as such
No matter how much I reload
Nothing remotely similar comes to sight
Increasing my anxiety with every night

I self-doubt
I internally shout to the sky
I beg for some kind of divine intervention
Or maybe that time traveling invention

To see what will become of me in the impending years
Will I be surrounded by cheers?
Or will I be drowning in tears?

Will I have a purpose?
Will I have goals?
Will climbing off the bed in morning
Stop being like walking on coal?

Will I find love?
What if I lose it?
Will I have more friends?
Will I stop seeing myself as an object
Yet to mend?

So many questions
But none answered
Whenever I try to contact God
I'm always put on hold

Uncertainty and fear are the worst emotions
Sometimes I can't listen past my mind's commotion
I can't hear people's voices
I often overthink and later regret my choices.

So, about these voices
They just never shut up
They keep occupying my mind
Turning me into someone bitter instead of sweet and kind
And I starting to believe that in near future
My sanity might not be found

Good Night, Dorothea?

Dorothea was laying on the ground
Her hair is in a messy bun
Her bottle of alcohol
Oh dear, that she's already downed

She's going crazy
She's completely convinced
She just doesn't want to feel this pain
Sometimes she wonders if she could just drown in the rain

She laid on the ground
And frowned to her empty wine glass
She remembered her first day in class
Where everyone was someone's friend
She was that awkward and quiet kid
Other girls left her out
That made her internally shout

She shakes her head and dries off her tears
Well, what can one do
When everyone considers you mature for your age
Even your peers

She picks up the glass and throws it across the room
She goes to the dining table and starts to nibble on yesterday's leftover food

Then she remembered her
And cruel words
She said, "You don't feel any emotions!"
Dorothea stiffened
She went completely quiet and still
She shut herself off
But she could still hear her scoff

What's wrong with me?
She asked herself every night
Why can't I be a normal human being?
Why can't I not be the centre of attention
But still be seen!?!

She looks out the misted window
She saw the familiar swing
She remembered her grandfather used to swing her back and forth
He used to play with her without being bored
He saw the version of her that was innocent and when it was quiet in her head
When she could sleep in her bed

Tears clouded at that realisation
That the one person who truly could have loved and understood her was dead

That instead of sleeping
She has regular crying sessions in her bed

She looks at herself in the mirror
She almost doesn't recognise herself
The girl that was so put together
The girl who always had a plan
Now she maniacally laughs
And misses the days she spent in her pram

She was messed up
Inside - Out
She wonders will it be out of character for her if she shouts?
She dropped the thought
Since she had doubts

She goes back to bed
And stares at the ceiling
She wonders how did it come this?
She knew everything when she was young
Now she can't stop herself from pouring her heart out in the notes app
As if it's a drug

She frowned
It's midnight
She should be sleeping safe and sound
She should dream
Maybe that's where her better version can be found?

The What If Spiral

'I'm sorry, I can't do this anymore."
Said your suicide note
That you wrote
A chill pass through my spine
I saw you laughing the other day
I assumed you were fine!

Tears cloud my eyes
As I remember when the teacher broke the news
I remember feeling completely confused

You were the funniest little kid
You recommended movies that were inappropriate and wild
While you were going through something
You shouldn't have!
You were just a child!

I remember how much you joked
I remember you always had an audience for your show
I remember your sweet smile
Every memory of you is sitting in my 'it's going to haunt me for the rest of my life ' file

So, now I just stare at the ceiling of this dark room
Every day's topic of overthinking is 'What if I had just called you?'

So, you must've gathered as much
That I overthink and overanalyse a little too much
Every 'What if?' scenario in my head
Every sob, cry and dark thought is muffled in this bed

What if -
I had just called.
I had texted.
Would you have given life another chance
And instead, just bawled?

What if you had just bawled?
Your trouble
Your pain
Would you have been convinced that the sun always shows up after the rain?

What if you would have gotten convinced?
Would you have returned to school?
Would you have broken your cool and carefree mask?
Would you have just made a scene?
Would you have just screamed?

What if you had screamed?
Would you have released every one of your bottled-up emotions?

Would you have at least tried to share your mind's constant commotion?

I wipe my tears
And muffle my sobs
I try not to dwell much on these 'what ifs'
But grief has arrived
And it grips me so tight
But I have no energy left for a fight

I'm angry
I'm sad
I'm feeling emotions
I had no idea I was capable of feeling
I guess, I am just reeling

I'm still waiting for someone to say that it's just a bad dream
That I will wake up soon

I'm waiting for someone to tell me
That everything is alright
That you are happy, healthy, and alive
That you are still in that classroom, making jokes
That there is a complete me
And no part of me you broke

Behind Closed Doors

I'm going to make it, mum
I'm going to make it, dad
No matter how much it makes me sad

I'm going to make you proud
No matter how much self-doubt
Creeps into my mind
No matter if my better version is not yet found

I say these lines in the mirror
To myself
Wondering if they will help

I wonder if it would help a girl who is so beyond repair
Who cowers under their judgemental stares
She wonders if someone will even care
If she slips down the stairs?

Her ears hear a sound that no one else hears
She was a weirdo amongst her peers
She's so quiet and cute
They practically love her mute

They said she's mature for her age
They are oblivious to the mental cage
She keeps herself locked in
They chuckle and say she's got to have thicker skin

She tried not to take it by heart
But she failed time and time again
She used rain as a cover up for releasing her tears
For she believed that they couldn't know that she too had fears

They couldn't know that she even had emotions
They couldn't know about her mind's constant commotion
She barely survived life
She felt like she was working her ass off
But still there was no sight of promotion

They said you must have faith
As if it was easy
She never felt a divine connection to God
She chanted prayers that she never meant
She wondered if it's a sign of the beginning of the end

She struggled because of her low self esteem
She waited until everyone went to sleep
Then she internally screamed and sobbed
She grieved for the happier version of her
That was practically robbed

She stopped showing any emotions on her face
She never gave them anything
No trace
Of the hurt and pain, she felt everyday
She wondered if she's gone astray

She cared
She cared a little too much
About everyone's opinion on her
Her ears kept ringing
She could practically hear their taunts

They always said come out of the library
Come out of your books
Life's so beautiful
Come take a look

She wasn't interested in the so called 'beautiful' life
She wanted to remain in her novels, poems, and fables
Where she couldn't care about her being unstable
She could have a beginning, middle and end already written
She wondered what if in next life, she gets born as kitten!

Homecoming

Ravi texted 'Remember me, Sarge?'
That did something to our Pipa's poor heart
Tears clouded her eyes
As she fumbled for a response

Memories flashed through her mind
The good kind
Their Little Kilton days
Where they had so many demons to brave

She remembered how they were both a mess
When they met
Honestly, a little depressed

She said that she's going to solve the Andie Bell case
Together they went on adventures of their own
You can know all about it on 'The Good Girl's Guide to Murder' podcast on your phones

He was sunshine
She was midnight rain
They started as strangers
But a year ago
They parted ways with so much pain

She closed her eyes
And as she remembered his face
His black hair
He was so handsome
That it wasn't fair

She remembered how he always made her laugh
When there was light
But especially when it was dark

She remembered how he hugged her that night
When Stanley Forbes was killed
He loved her so much
He would have paid her therapy bills

She remembered their silent ways of saying ' I love you '
Their constant urge to touch each other
She remembered how good he was to her brother

She remembered how he wanted to protect her so bad
She remembered how he filled colours in her life so sad

She remembered how he rested his forehead against hers
How he fought the whole world just for her

She remembered him calling her 'Sarge'
How he clapped for her from the sidelines
As she was the star of the show
How when he kissed her
And she glowed

She glowed with that feeling
The one with wings
How his mere presence tugged at her heartstrings

They were a team
He used to say
They sticked together
No matter the weather

She remembered all the nicknames that he called her by
Her heart broke when she remembered
How they had to temporarily say goodbye

But now here she was
She and her phone
It's been a year
Yes, she's grown
But underneath she's a mess

Without Ravi, she's messed up and alone
So, when Ravi calls now
She smiles a teary smile
And answers the phone

I Hate You! (No, I Don't)

They say good things come to those who wait
But I am tired of leaving everything up to fate
They tell me to have faith
That it has no expiration date
Tell this to my soul, yet to sate

They say- "You really thought that all your dreams were going to come true?"
"Come on now, stop being so optimistic"
"Start being realistic!"

They say cruel things, one second
And go back to joking, the other
They are good at this
This realisation makes me shudder

They say you're going to get married
And have kids
You're going to be just like us
You're going to do exactly what we said and did
Well, shit.

They say- "You don't have any clue how lucky you are!"
"You're being handed whatever you want!"

But little do they know
That this pain in my chest grows
Every day
But when they say things like this
I don't know what to say

They say - "Be grateful!"
"For you have a roof over your head!"
"For you sleep in a warm bed!"

But little do they know about my conversations with the ceiling
The nights where I am just reeling
Good days and bad
In the end, when I reach the bed
I just feel sad

They don't care about my screams and sobs
They only care that I get a nine to five job
They don't care about broken dreams
They don't care that you feel as if my happiness has been robbed

They don't care when self-doubt creeps into my mind
They don't care about the manuscripts that I hide
They don't care about the notes app that keep locked
Or about the stash of candy, I always keep stocked

They say grow a little taller
Lose some weight

They are the reason I still fear weighing scales
Believe me, I have seen some horrific days

I hide
And I admit
Ever since I was a kid

I hide every imperfection
I hide every scar
I hide far in the corner
So, you wouldn't see
The real me

The real me is a mess
I feel everything
But keep it suppressed
And I don't appreciate you jokingly calling me depressed

I hate that I act and behave like someone else
I hate that I am an ornament, you keep on the shelf
That you ignored my calls of help

I hate that maybe I am the only one who sees
These lines and walls rising from the ground
Slowly and gradually

I hate that we are not what we were
I hate that we are slowly growing apart
But I hate the way it's breaking my heart

Lost and Seeking

I stalk in my dark room
And look at the sky
I assume God is looking at me
As I say that we need to talk

Life isn't what it was supposed to be
I was supposed to be free
Free of feeling like I'm drowning everyday
That I'm on edge when someone simply says 'Hey'

They say - Life's like a box of chocolates
You're never going to know what you're going to get'
Then when I worry
They tell me not to fret

They say that you exist
That you're watching over us from the sky
Do you really?
Then why don't you see how hard I try?

Tell me, even after trying so much
Why I don't succeed?
Why do I want to go back to being a seed?

Small, protected and yet to grow
Yet to be judged based on every little flaw

Tell me why do I feel so lost?
Why do I feel so hollow?
Why does it become so hard to swallow?

They ask me to develop some faith
They say good things come to those who wait
They say that we have an already written fate
I say nothing
I just nod mechanically
I stiffen

They ask me to surrender my future to you
And I start looking for their missing screw
Because I can't seem to let go of myself
Do they have a diagnosis for this state?

No God, just tell me
Do I even get a happy ending?
Or do I continue to rot?
In the same old me
Who silently cries and equally silently screams

Come on God, give me a hint
Will these nightmares of being a failure are ever going to end?
Am I going to peacefully sleep in my bed?

Oh God, you must spill
Will I live a life and feel fulfilled?
Am I ever going to live my dream?
Will I ever hope?
Will I ever dream?

Dear God, what's your take?
What is true happiness?
Is it earning a million dollars
Or your favourite chocolate cake?

Come on God, you must tell
How many times I'll fall?
And how many times will I pick myself up?
Will everyone still think I'm okay?
Or will they finally call my bluff

Life's tough, I get it
No one said that it's going to be easy
But please tell me that it will get easier one day
When will I stop fantasizing about disappearing into outer space?
Tell me that I will find a safe space
To let it all out
A place where I'll finally be found

A Dreamer's Manifesto

I open my threads app
And see many authors saying
"Hey. I woke up as a published author."
I smile and say to myself that someday that's going to be me

One day I'll have a thousand books
Whose spine would have my name
An 'About the Author' page on the back
That will say read what goes on the mind of this sad sack

One day I'll create characters- messy, complicated and will be anything but fine
They'll have their dad's anger issues
My readers will have to bring their own tissues

My stories and poems will make them laugh
They will make them cry
And that will be the motivation for me to try
Even though I don't see a future for me in sight

I'll make my characters fall in love
They'll separate
But they'll end up together in the end

Some of my characters will die
That might make me and my readers cry
Because those characters will leave their mark
One story must end for the next story to start

I'll create characters who would make my readers laugh
But beware! Their sense of humour is just their mask
To hide their broken homes
Their dark pasts
But they'll manage to capture our hearts

I'll create complicated familial relationships
Messy and doomed college trips
Complex love triangles
Oh yes, they'll read all about the juicy scandal

Some friendships will break
There will be lovers who hate each other's guts
There will be friends who secretly harbour their feelings
At the time of climax, all these characters will be reeling

There will be healthy relationships, of course
A mother who fights for her child
The main character allowing herself to be wild
The 'Chosen One' for once will be treated like a child

The princess will elope with the notorious rake
They'll create a life of their own
They'll make their own wedding cake

The nerdy girl in me who was bullied in school
In my books, her character will break all rules
She won't be the sad sack that I am
She won't give anyone a damn
About anyone's opinion
She won't give them the power to make her feel inferior

There will book signings and meet and greets
I'll create a newsletter where I'll post about my future books and their sneak peeks
Teenage girls will find solace in my imagination
They'll read books even on vacation

Fulfilling my dreams will take my blood, sweat and tears
It will take overcoming my fears
Of not being good enough
Of not being able to survive in this life, so tough

People around me would be proud
In my books, I'll be found
My nine-year-old self will be safe and sound
In between these pages
She'll be out of her mental cages
She'll be happy one day
Even if it takes ages

Whispers of a Weary Heart

Don't put dreams into my head
If they won't come true
Why couldn't you have picked a different colour?
Why did you colour my soul only in blue?

I ask, as I gaze into the sky
Wondering if it grimaces when it hears my helpless cries
My muffled sobs and sighs
Does it comment- "Well, at least she tried."

I gaze at the sky with tears in my eyes
Wondering if it ever sighs
I wonder if it gets tired of me and my complaints
I wonder if it has any cure for this pain

I avert my gaze
And stare at my hands
I close my eyes
I try to focus on my uneven sighs

I think time really slips like sand
How can things go quickly so out of hand?
I try to think how life became so complicated
Since when did I start feeling so unsated?

Since when did I get so high strung?
Since when do I have issues that need to be debunked?
Since when did I get so lost when everything once was crystal clear?

How did I become such a messed-up kid?
Who sees a dress she likes and wonders if she'll fit.

Since when did my midnights become my afternoon?
Since when do I give company to the moon?
Whereas other young ladies might swoon and croon
I overthink my entire future, right in the early June

Since when did I feel like a loser?
Since when did I feel like a beggar rather than a chooser?
Since when did I crave ice cream so much?
I guess, you can always count on a tub of Belgium chocolate, when life gets tough

Since when do I dig my own graves?
Since when did I start believing that no one stays?
That everyone in my life is going to leave somehow
But why?
I'm me, that's how

Questions, Questions
There are a lot of them
No answers found, yet
I wonder to myself every night in bed

Anyway, you haven't answered me yet
I look at the sky as I ask
Does providing a cheat sheet to get through life, is such a difficult task?

I mean I've asked you a million times
But you haven't answered
Does it mean that my call got transferred?

Are you secretly giggling and chortling
While listening to my pain?
Wondering how to make this more of an interesting game
And saying - "Look at her go again, I wonder how much more can she be chained."
But I keep pouring my heart out
Same old same

Secrets Behind Silence

I try to calm myself
I try to steady my trembling hands
As I sit on the bathroom floor
Gosh! I'm out of breath

You're fine
You're fine
I mutter to myself
This is my version of asking for help

I try to steady uneven breaths
I try to tell myself not to fret
And yet
My muscles remain locked
Due to the secret, I've been keeping for so long

It embarrasses me
It scares me a lot
When someone touches me whenever they want

A simple touch on shoulders
My world goes a little colder

I wish I could tell someone about that night
The night that physical touches became my source of fright

Yes, I remember every day and every night
I've tried to forget all about it
But I fail and fail again
I'm not sure how I feel sane

They say "Relax your body and just let go"
But my mind and body didn't get the memo
They grow frantic and panicked by every second
I go back to that night where I was helpless
And had no weapon

I had nothing to protect myself
I couldn't scream for help
He apologized then
And said that it was a mistake
But after all these years I can still feel the ache

The ache of being physically violated
That he touched me without my consent
I'm drowning in suffocation
But I have no place to vent

I remember how mean he was to me
How he mocked my every breath
He criticized my every move

I want to just move on
But I just can't fucking move!

So, I try to live my boring and simple life
I try to smile at the jokes that aren't funny
I try not to take offence to their painful jibes
Courtesy of the typical Indian wives

Someone said Indian families have changed
Of course, that person turned out to be insane
Because he has no idea about the pain
He has no idea about the mental chains
This constant feeling of disdain

He doesn't know about gender discrimination
He doesn't know about the judgement in their stares
And believe me, they scare
They scare the little girl in me
They creep out the teen me
As an adult, I just mentally flip them off
I keep my face stoic and my emotions off

I carry this bitterness inside
As I paste a smile to hide
Every scar
Every secret of mine
They'll never know the truth
Not until I stop to shine

Heartstrings and Harmony

I give you my scarf
And I ask you to give it back next time
You beam as if I just gave you my heart

It is the start of a love story
He is warm, funny, and kind
He is indeed one of his kind
I am moody, guarded, and bland
Who am I?
Don't worry, no one really understands

We were strangers before
And now we hope we're something more
I wonder how life could become this
This constant state of heavenly bliss

What is Love, anyway?
Is it the wild set of butterflies?
Or the condition of being on all fours?
Is it flowers and grand romantic gestures?
Is it based on a person's complexion?

Or maybe Love is just hormonal releases and brain chemicals being triggered?
Or maybe it just doesn't exist?
There are various theories
You get the gist

But what if Love is just being weird together?
What if Love is becoming better together?
Maybe it's all the arguments and fights?
Maybe it isn't about who's wrong and who's right?
Maybe it's being completely and totally being with someone no matter how many obstacles in
sight?

Love isn't about grand candlelight dinners
It isn't about saints or sinners
It isn't about drowning or falling
And for some people, crawling

Love is just putting the other person's needs on the front seat
When just the thought of being near them
makes your body heat
When you want that person all to yourself
When they save you from yourself

Love is being intimate with a person you never knew you could be
Love can feel like drowning

Love can set you free
Each day in love feels like a new dream

Love can break you
Love can heal
Love has such power to bring a person to their knees

Love is hand holding
Love is passionate kisses
Love is fulfilling the other person's secret wishes

Love can feel like a warm hug
Love can feel like you've been stung
It doesn't matter if you're carefree or high strung
As long as you're in love
You're always drunk

Love can make you mad
Love can make you sad
It can make you see only that one person in a crowd
Love has the power to finish all self-doubt

Love has the power to kiss all the insecurities away
Love can make you feel
Love can make you grin like a fool
Love can make you realise there is more to life than wealth
Love makes you value health

Love gives you the comfort of the lullaby as sung your mother when you were little
But be careful!
Love is delicate
Love is brittle
Love is being completely smitten

Love can break you
And build you back up
Love can be soft
It can also be rough

Love sees no gender
Love teaches to never bend
To society
To the world
Love can be peace
But it might leave you exhausted and burnt

Love, no matter, it's type
It happens to all of us
No matter how much we call the concept overhyped
Love can be an endgame
Love can be incomplete
But without love, us humans will deplete

The Burden of Being

She aimlessly walks
She doesn't really talk
Although she is the talk of the town
People talk about her eye rolls and frowns

She wears a stained crown on her head
She's got head full of things best left unsaid
She's got eyes full of tears best left unshed
She's angry when she isn't fed

Her mental health hangs on by a thread
She psychoanalysis herself in her childhood bed
Beware! She's insane
She's got her emotions chained

She's trained herself to keep it all inside
She goes under her bed to hide
Her secrets
Her pain
She's got demons to tame behind her demeanour so plain

Her mind never stops
There is this constant noise in her head
She sobs and cries about it in her bed

She constantly listens to Taylor Swift
She barely exists
In this reality
In this world
She lies in her bed hollow and burnt

She doesn't like confrontation
She's sick of her desperation
Her mind constantly works with no vacation

She listens to sad songs for fun
Yes, you heard it right
Don't look back just, run!

She loses herself in melancholic hymns
You can say, she's a bit grim
She sings without an audience
And let me tell you, this girl sings

She thinks a lot about Wendy and Peter Pan
She wonders what they could have become
If only Peter Pan didn't run away from commitment
If only he wasn't so dumb

She's addicted to colours beige, brown and lavender
She's never been an attacker, always a defender

She remembers almost everything
The guy who touched her inappropriately

The middle school bullies who intimidated her with their stares
The nights she cried and screamed at the sky and - 'It's not fair!'

She wants to live in bookshelves
Hiding between romance and self help
Where she can get lost all the time
Where she can truly be herself
Where escaping reality won't be such a big crime

She's never been the one who prays
She only felt hollow inside
She doesn't allow herself to confide
About her insecurities
About her dreams
About her nightmares
About her muffled screams

No one truly knows her, of course
She's always been a girl who wins bronze
Oh, but how much she wants to be awarded gold
She wants to write what she wants and not what she's told
She wants to be brave and bold
She wants to live a life before she gets old

Brainstorms and Heartaches

"When were you the happiest?"
My therapist asked
I shifted in my seat
Hoping she couldn't hear my increasing heartbeat

I remember being young
But never acting or feeling like my age
I was too clueless and oblivious to my mental cage

She asked me, "What is the wildest memory as a child?"
I shrugged
As I struggled to find a memory of being me just a child

She asked, "So, what were you as a child?
Don't hold back. Don't leave a single detail behind?"
I blew a ragged breath
Because where could I even start?
How could I even unload everything piled up in her
heart?

I was quiet
I was kind
I was labelled 'rare to find'

I was shy
I was reserved
I was loved as I deserved

My nose was always buried in a book
I loved to escape
My ability to articulate started to fade
My ability to feel started having an expiry date

Each day as I grew up
I started to doubt everything in my past
I realised that any moment spent with a loved one could be the last

I lost
I gained
I treated myself with disdain

I have everything
So probably I don't know the actual concept of pain
I can't see the path ahead
Even though the bridge of my nose is under the specs frame

She analysed
She absorbed
Every piece of information she got
About each day I felt hollow and distraught

I told her that I've tried to cry
I even carry my own tissues
But the tears just don't come out
Sometimes I just internally shout

And sometimes it gets hard to pretend
With family and friends
That everything is okay
I am fine
That my golden wheels aren't rusting
They still shine

I don't know if I like this version of me
Chained and held back in my mind
When people tell me I'm 'one of a kind'
All I want is to hide
In my room
Where no one will question why I am so gloom
Or why do I feel like I'm going to die soon?

Inner Dialogue

I'm in a love and hate relationship with my thoughts
They're a mess
Yet to sort

I love it here
But I hate it even more
Sometimes in the middle of the night
You can find me shattered on the floor

Every night, my thoughts run wild
Hurting and belittling my inner child
For being so...so...I don't honestly know why
But I do end up crying

At some point, I realise that I can't breathe
I press my face in a pillow and muffle my screams
I pray for even nightmares
Because I know better than to hope to dream

I feel like drowning in a deep sea
I'm underwater
I scream
But I feel myself fade
Is this going to get worse with age?

My mother asks me why I hold back
Why do I have to be a sad sack?
She tells me to talk more and be more frank
But I know that ship already sank

My brother bothers me a lot
He's become a teenager, you know
So, I've got to listen to his mean quips
And just ignore

He says I'm dumb
That I'm high strung
That I can't do anything right
That I'm practically mute
Don't you dare say what he says is cute

I think of my older siblings
And my heart breaks
My heart aches
Because they're leaving one by one
Leaving me in our childhood home, undone

They'll all leave
One by one
I fear that I'll be here all alone
Picking up my broken pieces in my childhood home

You don't know what it's like to overanalyse every move
and every sigh

Of everyone that surrounds you
And you have no idea how much of them they show is true

But it's the nights that hit me hard
It's just me and mind
And believe me my thoughts are far from kind

There is this constant buzz in my mind
A lot of questions
And answers yet to find
And I hope
I just hope one day this world becomes a little kind

There Within the Stars

Did it really get easier?
In the sky, you reside
Where you don't have to hide
Yourself behind a mask

Did you find peace?
Did you find happiness?
Did you finally release your emotions, suppressed?

No, tell me
Did it really get easier?
Up there in the sky?

Do you hear your mother's muffled sobs?
Do you also feel the grief she carries because of the child
she was robbed of?
She stopped smiling
She stopped feeling at all
Do you have the urge to reach her out?
Do you wish you could hear her shout?

Do you see your childhood friends break?
Do you maybe have the urge to do something to spare
them from this ache?

Does your heart break?
When you see them drown in grief
Trust me, grief's visit isn't brief

Do you see your little brother?
With whom you shared so many memories
Now with you gone he's become so grim
His light has become dim

Do you feel your father's tears?
How he's living his worst fears?
He lost his son
He lost his best friend
Now his heart's broken in a way
That no one can mend

We've read your suicide note a thousand times
And yet it makes every time shed tears
It said just one line
I cannot bear to repeat
Sometimes I wish I could bury myself six feet under deep

Did you experience the childhood that you didn't have?
Did you finally regain the innocence that was trapped?
Did you finally try to genuinely smile?
Did you finally find the courage to be yourself?
Did you finally learn to ask for help?

Did you ever regret your decision?
Did you ever regret what you did?
Did you feel like you've disappointed your version as a kid?

Did you miss the life that you lived?
Being someone's brother, friend, and kid
Or were you relieved from the weight of the responsibility
To be free of this burden so much?
That made you take a decision so tough

Do you maybe think you could've said more
In the suicide letter you left?
That left us reeling and bereft
Did you have something to say that got left?

There within the stars
Did you finally heal your scars?
Did you find the comfort you couldn't find here?
For which you decided to leave everyone you considered dear

There within the stars, did you find yourself helpless
To not be able to hug everyone visiting your grave
Where they wonder what more could they have given to keep you here
What more they could have done to make you see your future clear

There within the stars
Did you finally find a way to heal your scars?
Did you finally find a way to be the perfect brother,
friend, and son?
Did you ever regret what you've done?

You can't run
To your childhood home
Or have a journey towards growth
Or a life fulfilled and fully lived to the fullest
For now, you can only rest

Commotion Within

It's day- I don't know because I've lost count
I'm personified self-doubt
I wonder if this is how it's always going to be
Please someone tell me it's a dream

Sometimes I find myself
Aimlessly sitting in my car
I've already counted the passing cars
I've gazed at the shooting stars

I think and I think
Because that's all I supposedly do
I wonder if there are any signs that I grew

You see, I am a person without a purpose in sight
Not even in my dreams
I've even stopped to daydream

I've become this hollow person from inside
I've become this girl who just hides
Pretty much every part of herself
No one can hear my muffled sobs of help

I've got this noise permanently living in my head
This volume seems to increase when I lay in bed

I ponder
About all the things unsaid
The constant commotion in my head
About my sanity hanging by a thread

I try to think of a bright future for myself
But not too much
Since dreaming is easy
Converting the dream into reality is tough

I ponder over questions such as - What is Life?
I wonder how it would feel to be stabbed by a knife
How the blood would gush out
How would I even react?
Would I even shout?

I think about sexuality
I think about burned cigarette buds
I think about the setting sun
I think about all the challenges I'll have to face
Before I come undone

I think about the people that are going to leave me behind
Or how many times I'll alter the definition of people
being kind?
How many times will I be lost when I don't even know
what to find?

I feel too much at the same time
It made me scared to express
I flinch even at the smallest physical contact
That's the only time I don't overthink before I act

Tomorrow is going to be yet another day
I'm desperate to find some colour in life, so grey
I hope to find the path I am meant to walk on
I sometimes wonder why I was even born

Six Months and Counting I Remember

It's been six months two hours and thirty minutes
Since you left
Leaving me here reeling and bereft

I can still picture your face brightened up
Every time we danced in the rain
The memory almost eases some of the pain

I remember how we tried to make each other laugh
On our bad days
How we both added colour to our life, so grey

I remember your warm embrace
I remember your familiar face
I remember all the nights you held me tight
When I was scared that I had no future in sight

You recited positive affirmations in my ears
You kissed all my silent tears
You caressed all my fears
And for a moment
Everything was crystal clear

I remember all the nights I spent in your embrace
All the obstacles that we faced
I've been stuck in this hedge maze every day
You never fade

I remember your blue eyes
They were a tough competition to the sky
Your dimples on both the cheeks

I remember your warm smile
I remember your every breath
I remember holding onto each part of you
When we were already dead

You always wake up from your dreams
And realise it wasn't real
That's how I feel

It's been six months two hours and thirty minutes
Since you've left
And ever since that day I've been the same
Depressed and lost is how I exist everyday

It's been a load of tears
A load of buried fears
My heart breaks
My heart aches
But don't worry, I smile, even though it's fake

I remember
And I remember
Because that's all I seem to do
Every morning, I zone out while the coffee brews

I don't know how to be who I used to be before you
I don't know how to move ahead
Or to stop crying in my bed
Or to stop craving for your touch
Yeah, these couple of months have been rough

So, come here and tell me
How to move on?
How to be that version of me that's long lost gone?
How to make this pain go away?
How to be someone who can make people stay?
Come on, for god's sake, come here
And tell me I am going to be okay

Seasons of Seperation

I sat in that restaurant
I told my friends that I was okay
They stared knowingly at me a beat longer than required
And that's all it took my heart to break

My expression caved
My smile slipped
I broke down in tears
In short, I made a scene
If I wasn't being crystal clear

For the very first time I didn't care
About their hushed whispers and judgemental stares
All I could think was that you both would be gone in a matter of months
And then what!?!
We'll be over and done!??

The other day I was sitting by the window and remembered our summer days
I remembered our carefree days
When we had no dreams and targets to chase
Can't we go back to that place?

I remembered how we assembled that plastic tent
And we didn't have to pay any kind of rent
We could've lived in that cramped up tent forever
Just being there together made everything better

The other night, I cried
As if someone had died
I guess something did die
Our innocence and the days when we were just a child

I recalled our muffled laughter in the dark
How we played hide and seek in the park
How we ate custard and strawberry jelly all day
Oh, how I wish we could return to that place!

The other day, I was cleaning the attic
I found old photographs of when we were just kids
When we had no responsibilities over our heads
The days when we peacefully slept in our childhood beds

In those old photographs
We made weird faces
We were embarrassing as hell
We were laughing at jokes
That none of us can re tell

Dear older sister
Do you remember how our brother used to chase us down the street?

How he made us cry?
And then made us stop by bribing us with sweets!

We really did grow up, didn't we?
From being innocent and carefree
To making our own decisions
And walking alone in streets
From stressing over school exams
To trusting God's plans

We really were something, weren't we?
We were a trio
It was just us three

I knew that you both were going to leave the nest, one day
But I didn't expect you both to leave me behind
Leaving me undone and frozen in our childhood bed
Where I reel and overthink everything, we left unsaid

And I know this is probably goodbye for good
That we'll be separated
No matter the weather
I hate that we're separating and taking different roads
I hate that everything is changing
I hate that one day we'll all be gone
And that we've moved out and moved on from our pillow fort

I Hate It

I hate it
I hate waking up every day
I hate when I'm quiet
I hate when everything gets worse when I say

I hate my arms
I hate my thick thighs
I hate that I feel so empty
Yet I can't seem to cry

I hate my face
I hate that everyone except me is ahead in this rat race
And they all move forward with their aim
Meanwhile I am just the same

I hate my straight black hair
I hate that everyone misunderstands my inability to express and say- "She doesn't even care!"

They call me names behind my back
They criticize my every flaw, every crack
They say - "Learn to take a joke!"
They have no idea of how much of me they broke

Every joke
Every jibe
It hurts me in a way
I can't even describe

I hate that I endure it all
I hate phone calls
I hate that everyone has grown tall
Or maybe it's just my downfall

I hate that when they ask- "When did you last smile?"
I can't seem to recall
I can't seem to recall when I truly smiled
I have always been this way, even as a child

I hate that I don't know if I am a good person or not
I hate that I bear the guilt of breaking hearts
Because I couldn't say the right thing
I hate that my words are only meant to sting

They call me 'the old mean grandma' at my face
I can read their gaze
That says - "What a disgrace!!!"

I hate it inside my head
I hate all my thoughts
I hate that if my younger version sees me now, she'll be extremely distraught

I hate that my brain works this way
Either I am quite
Or I always have the worst possible thing to say
But you know, aside from that
I'm okay!

I hate my every body part
I hate everything I feel
I sometimes want to peel off my skin
I hate all the misery, I seem to spill

I suck the oxygen in every room
I am personified gloom
I hate and I hate
Because that's all I seem to do
I wonder if I'll ever attain happiness that's completely true

Will I ever look at my family and smile?
Will I ever be as carefree as a child?
Will I ever let my guard down?
Will I forever frown?
Oh God, just tell me!
Will I ever be happy!?!
Will I ever open the jar that contains my emotions, suppressed
Sincerely, a nineteen-year-old (utterly depressed!)

Inhale, Exhale

Inhale
Exhale
Every breath of mine
Reminds me of how terribly I failed

"Failed at what?" Someone in my head asks
I get sometimes like this in the dark
"Failed at every relationship, everything that I ever tried!"
I replied

"Explain a little more." That imaginary being asked
again
And I wonder if I'm ever going to become sane
I rub my face with my clammy hands
I don't bother fixing my messed-up hair

"You see, I am not the pleasant person that I used to be
once I was young"
"Once I was picture perfect, now I am just high strung."
I imagine the imaginary thing tilting it's head
Which makes me blurt out all the things I had left unsaid

"I was, once perfect, quiet and every parent's dream child, only to grow up as someone who wonders when she's going to die"
"I am someone who never achieves something, no matter how much I try."

"I have this noise in my head that doesn't seem to die down, so I write all of it on paper."
"And wear this noise as a crown"

"I feel empty, angry and bitter all at the same time."
"But when someone asks, 'how I'm doing?', the answer's always 'I'm fine.'"

I toss and turn in my bed
I imagine the imaginary thing in my head doing the same
Trying to figure me out like it's a game

"There is this heaviness in my chest, which doesn't seem to go."
"No matter how many motivational quotes I read or how much I try to let go."

"I don't know what the future holds, apparently it's untold."
"It's like a manuscript, not even nearly ready to be sold."

"I don't like things that aren't in my control."
"I hate the things that are in my control, yet I fail at those things."

"The frustration and exhaustion of it all makes me say
things that are aimed to sting."

"It's like I don't know if I am a good person or not."
"I don't know if in the next five years, my mental health
will be like lush greenery or like a horrible drought"
The imaginary thing rolls its eyes at my imagination
Forgetting it's the only source of its creation

"Anyway, my point is that nothing feels right, in this
world black, grey and white."
"I don't see a bright future for myself in sight."
"I don't know how to make this situation right"

Inhale
Exhale
I will try it all again
Hoping one day it will ease this constant pain
I wonder if it will ever get better, like everyone says
Or will I forever be nineteen, alone and astray.

The Home You Left Behind

The room is empty
Where you once lived
And the superhero cups you sipped

Your music system is nowhere to be seen
And for the first time your room is completely clean
Your clothes and your favourite pillow are
packed in a suitcase
Because you're leaving
And you've got dreams to chase

You're leaving
And it's a fact
I want you to be happy
So, I will let myself be sad

Your superhero cape
Call your name again and again
It's naive
It doesn't know
That for you to grow
You must go

Your favourite ice cream shop
Still resides on that old, battered street
It still remembers when you were just three feet
And when you ran through the doors for the first time, carefree

Your childhood bed
Where you shed all the things, unsaid
Will keep your secrets safe
It won't tell a soul
No matter how much you grow

The markings on the wall
Which measured how much you've gotten tall
Will always be a proof that you indeed have grown
No matter how much you rise
No matter how much you fall

Your fairy wings
That monkey that you won at the carnival
That made the most atrocious sound
Tries to find you in every corner of your childhood home
But that version of you can never be found

The sunny day
The summer sun
Misses the days when life was just fun

Cycles and plastic tents
Are stored somewhere
As they gather dust
Now they have an additional metaphorical layer of rust

Every wall that you have painted
Every wall on which you have drawn
The floor where you once crawled
Weep silently as they watch you go
As they love you so
They try to let you go

But they aren't successful, you see
Because no matter where you go
You're everywhere here
You are in the things you hated
You are in the things you considered dear

These walls and these chairs
Remember every game of truth and dare
And now they all stare at the door
Waiting for you to walk through it
To come back home
And just visit

They remain here waiting with your mom and dad
They're getting old too
Never forget that

They wait from dusk to dawn
Whenever life brings you to your knees
Remember the porch light is always on

That Giddy Feeling

I know it's silly
I know it's just an adrenaline rush
But believe me when I say this
You are the only thing I look forward to in this life so rough

It's weird to be honest
It's honestly rough
I can't control my emotions around you
It scares the shit out of me
And my soul, so blue

We're completely opposite people
With different hobbies and interests
You're into sports and Olympics
And my daily newspaper is my Pinterest

You always sit in the back
I always sit in the middle or front
In my dreams I will tell you how I feel
I promise, I'll be upfront

We sit in different lanes
We have different social games
But I believe deep down we're the same

We've laughed
We've exchanged glances
I wonder if you behave like this with everyone
Or you're just oblivious to my involuntary advances

I am not saying that we could be a thing
Or grab me and put on a ring
But do you have that same giddy feeling in your mind?
Or is it just my imagination going wild?

I've liked people before
But I have never felt this way
Where I want you to know I feel
But I just can't say!

I can't be casual
I can't be just friends
Or whatever is the trend

I'm a hopeless romantic by heart
But I don't know where to start
I don't have a guide stating - beginning, middle and end
Am I still redeemable?
Or broken beyond mend?

It's crazy that we're in the same room
But you have no idea of the giddy feeling in my mind
I don't know how to stop blushing
Or stifle this stupid smile!

I lose sleep
I forget to eat
I pick my nails with my teeth
I overthink everything

Every smirk
Every smile
God, I'm such a child!

I'm nineteen
But nowadays I behave like I'm nine
So someday come here and read my mind
Read every thought, every dark secret I've stored
Take your time, make a decision

Tell me if I have indeed gone mad
Or humour me and tell me you feel the same way
Tell me you've seen all of me
And yet you will stay

Tell me that you will give me a story worthy of a romance novel
That whenever we fight, you'll happily throw the towel
You'll love my little quirks

You'll be patient and help me figure out how this thing works
Because I will be scared to death
Promise me you'll love me until your last breath

The Silent One

There were signs everywhere
It was in the little things she did
Because ever since she was born
She has never been just a kid

She locked her father in his room
She kept her brother at an arm's length
She never opened up to her mother
She never told her how she really felt

She was granite
She was dynamite
To be honest, she was more bark than bite
She always held back in a fight

She would overthink
She would over care
She would overthink and over care whenever she would over share
She believed that life was never fair

She was always stone faced
Her friends called her a girl boss
She related to Sylvia Plath and Robert Frost

She would read lots and lots of books
Because they don't flash her any judgemental looks
She would escape from this dreadful world
Where was peaceful and calm
Where she never let herself repeatedly burn

She wrote words and tried to make some sense
She never wanted to hurt anyone
She was just bleeding on paper
About the bonds that will never mend

She would write of her pain
She would write of her tears
She would write of her greatest fears
She dedicated her blood, sweat and tears into writing
That's the only thing that she believed to be exciting

She was uptight
She would never let her hair down
She would wear a permanent frown
Her wheels had become rusted and brown

She had built a wall around herself
So strong that no one could hear her own shouts of help

She tortured herself on a daily basis
She stopped trusting familiar faces

Her spectacles and braces
Symbolised that she had parts of herself yet to mend
She had nothing to call her own
She believed that she'll never fully grow

So why bother with a future anyway!?
She thought
When no one was going to eventually stay
Because she always had the worst possible thing to say

She wasn't perfect
She was more than aware
But she never knew how to show people that she too
cared!

She was strong on the outside
Inside?
She had a tender heart that felt too much
But expressed so less
She had gotten her personality suppressed

She cared about what people thought of her
Probably too much
But she used bitter words and silence as shields

Cinderella After Midnight

That little girl is all grown up now
She's finally learnt to bottle up her shouts
She blends herself in crowds
Thinking someday she will be found

She's become the Cinderella of their own life
She's started going out
And sneaking back into the house by midnight

She's stopped looking at the mirror and mimicking -
'Mirror, mirror, who's the fairest of all?'
She's started using it for pointing out all her cracks and flaws

She's upset with Rapunzel because 'She can't see the light' and 'She's got no dream'
She buries her head in their pillow and screams

She's stopped watching fairy tales
She's just counted the number of times
She's failed
Sometimes, to not lose
It's better to never set sail

She's thrown out her fairy wings
She's forgotten to sing
Songs of hope, bravery, and magic
She declared her life is tragic

She's outgrown
Winnie the Pooh
Winnie was her very first friend
But he can't fix parts of her yet to mend

And the magic wand has disappeared
She wishes that she could have it back
Maybe it would make her anxiety disappear
And maybe she'll forget all her fears

She's got a messed up mental state
She's stopped believing in things like fate
Sometimes she just wants to go back being eight
When life was easy to live
And no part of her ached

She misses the time
When she didn't have to fake
The smile that she wears
She misses the time
When she believed in the power of prayers

The girl who loved glitter
Has become bitter

She's become ugly and full of hate
She's got this heart that can easily break

Her spirit is already crushed
And people ask her
Why do you want to grow up so fast!?!
What's the rush!??

From the days of sugar rush
To experience adrenaline rush
From playing with plastic toys
To become a toy for boys

She's really grown up, I swear
But she never smiles anymore
She just permanently wears this glare
And don't stare into her eyes
She'll turn you into stone
Indeed, she really has grown

A Friend That Never Was

I am sitting on the bathroom floor
Yeah, I am not blind
I can see the ajar door
And you say that they're waiting for me
Yeah, sure!

And I stand up and walk outside the door
Only to find my 'so-called' friends laughing at me, curled up on the floor
And I feel like crying as if I'm still four

I go back to my seat
I open my lunch
Only to find that I don't want to eat

I torture myself by looking at the back seats
They're laughing
They're cracking jokes
Oblivious to all the promises they broke

And I don't celebrate friendship days
Because everyone makes promises
But no one stays
And they aren't worthy to be chased

I am probably that weird loner anyway
But I can hear them muttering
Is she naturally so silent?
Or is she just plain arrogant, who can say?

So, I remain on my seat, alone
Sitting there, rigid as stone
Pretending to be texting someone that doesn't exist
They forgot about me so Swift

And when they ask about us
I say that we've drifted apart
How do I tell them that how could we end
When we didn't even start?

And there are other people, I know
But it's hard for me to go
And start a conversation
God, I reek of desperation!

And I am the picked up last in every team
"Choose me, goddamn it!"
Will you listen
If I start to scream?

I am the spare one for you
I'm the note maker or the person who always has glue
No one talks to me
Unless they have something for me to do

I am not asking for gold or expensive stuff
All I am asking for is a friend
Who doesn't leave
When things get rough

I wait for someone to understand
Someone who keeps reaching out their hand
Who can help me stand
Who can make me walk through this life, so tough

Alas! I am talking to ghosts
My only companions who don't mind me as a host
I am still sitting on the bathroom floor again
But this time the door is closed